PaPeR CReatioNs

Joy Williams

NORTH LIGHT BOOKS

cincinnati, ohio
www.artistsnetwork.com

ABOUT THE AUTHOR

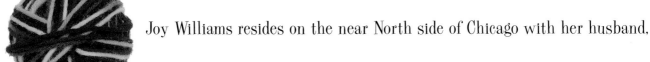

Joy Williams resides on the near North side of Chicago with her husband, Joel, and their newest addition, Pearl. Joy's unique creations reflect many years of teaching arts and crafts to urban children at summer camps along with directing art classes at an inner-city private school.

Joy finds her **inspiration** in the faces of her students.

The author at age 10!

Paper Creations. © 2002 by Joy Williams. Manufactured in China. All rights reserved. No part of this book may be reproduced in any form or by any electronic or mechanical means including information storage and retrieval systems without permission in writing from the publisher, except by a reviewer, who may quote brief passages in a review. Published by North Light Books, an imprint of F&W Publications, Inc., 4700 East Galbraith Road, Cincinnati, Ohio 45236. (800) 289-0963. First edition.

Other fine North Light Books are available from your local bookstore or art supply store or direct from the publisher.

06 05 04 03 02   5 4 3 2 1

Library of Congress Cataloging-in-Publication Data
Williams, Joy
    Paper Creations / by Joy Williams.
      p. cm.
    ISBN 1-58180-290-0 (alk. paper)
      1. Paper work–Juvenile literature. 2. Paper work. 3. Handicraft. I. Title
    TT870 .W54 2002
    745.54 21

                                            2001059064

Editors: Maggie Moschell and Kathi Howard
Cover Design: Andrea Short
Interior Design: Matthew DeRhodes
Layout Artist: Kathy Gardner
Production Coordinator: Mark Griffin
Photographer: Christine Polomsky

THANK YOU...

first of all, I want to thank God for allowing me to do what I enjoy most, sharing my art with children. Much, much thanks to my editor, Maggie Moschell, who has been such an encouragement and source of talent. Thanks to Debbie Baumgartner for her ideas and computer skills. Andrea Spicer—where do I begin? Jannelle Schoonover, my most wonderful sister, thanks for another belly full of laughs. Also thanks to my super parents, Royce and Carol Schoonover; the best in-laws, Vic and Katherine Williams; and Bethie Nicholls, Tammy Perlmutter, Tiana Clark, Deb Strahan, Corey Escue, Karen Warne, Marsha Spaniel, Eric Bixler, Kat Seiler, Georgia Coleman, all of the students at U.C.S. and my family and friends at J.P.U.S.A. for their support.

dedication

This book is dedicated to my husband, Joel,

and our Pearl of great price.

I love you both!

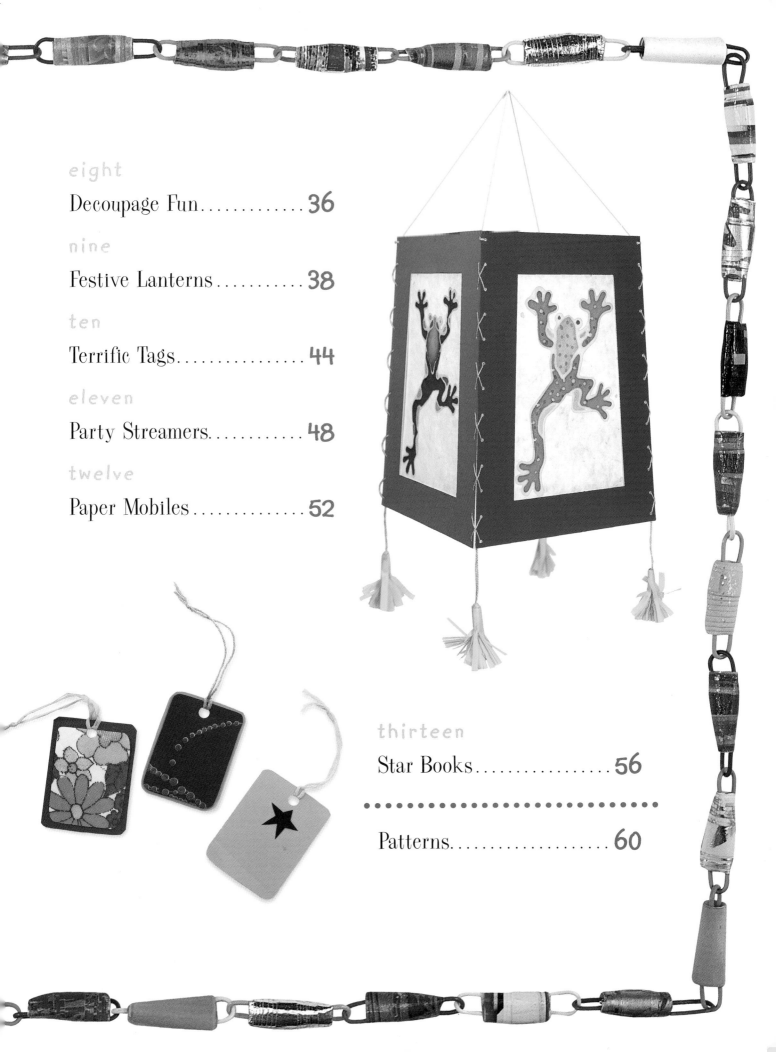

A NOTE TO GROWN-UPS

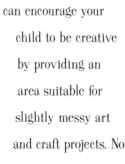

This is a collection of fun, kid-tested paper projects that will encourage your child to be creative. The step-by-step photos and simple instructions make it easy for your child to do these projects with little or no adult help. Best of all, each project will be unique because your child's own imagination is the most important ingredient.

Encouraging Budding Artists

Making art and craft projects helps develop a child's manual dexterity and problem-solving skills while offering the opportunity for imaginative, creative self-expression. You can encourage your child to be creative by providing an area suitable for slightly messy art and craft projects. No special equipment is needed, just a place to sit and a surface on which to work that can be wiped clean or covered with paper.

Easy access to art supplies will enable your child to do these activities whenever the mood strikes and to clean up afterward with just a little help from you. Art supplies can be stored in boxes under a cabinet or other accessible place so your child can take things out and put them away.

Collecting Supplies

The materials are easily found at drugstores, grocery stores or craft outlets, but it's not necessary to buy the paper for these projects. Help your child collect leftover wallpaper, old maps, candy wrappers, "junk mail," magazines, used gift wrap, paper napkins and other paper goods that you find around the house.

Children enjoy showing their loved ones the things they have made, and the praise they receive goes a long way toward keeping the creative spark alive for a lifetime.

BE A GOOD ARTIST

Art and craft projects can be messy. Cover your workspace with paper or a vinyl tablecloth.

Wipe up any spills right away and always clean up when you are finished.

Neatness counts! Keep your hands clean. Cut and fold the paper as neatly as you can. Your projects will look terrific!

When you use a glue stick, put scrap paper underneath your project to protect the table. Be sure you put glue all the way to the edges.

After you glue paper with a glue stick, rub the paper and count to ten until the glue sets.

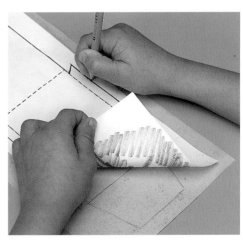

For projects that use patterns, trace or photocopy the pattern, cut it out, place it on your project and trace along the outside edges. Or you can use pencil to darken the back of the tracing or photocopy and then trace over the pattern to transfer it onto your project.

MATERIALS

The materials that are needed are shown at the beginning of each project. Here are descriptions of the things you will use for making the projects in this book.

COPIER PAPER

Computer, photocopier or typing paper comes in white, prints, and a rainbow of colors.

VELLUM

Vellum is translucent like tissue paper, but it's thicker and stiffer. Vellum is found in stores that sell scrapbooking supplies. **Tracing paper** is a good substitute for white vellum.

GIFT WRAP

Gift wrap comes in many exciting colors, patterns and prints. Many of the projects in this book can be made with scraps of used or leftover bits of wrapping paper.

TAGBOARD

This paper is called oaktag, cardstock or tagboard. It's thicker than writing paper but thinner than cardboard. File folders (in cream or bright colors) are a good substitute for tagboard.

CONSTRUCTION PAPER

Construction paper is a colorful, inexpensive, heavy paper that fades in sunlight.

TISSUE PAPER

Tissue paper is thin and translucent, which means you can see light through it. It comes in prints and solid colors.

OTHER PAPER

Craft stores sell **origami paper**, which comes in handy small squares and many different prints and colors. Paper for scrapbooking is also exciting and colorful. You can make thin paper stronger by gluing it onto paper cut from **paper bags**. Use it for projects that you sew with needle and thread. Thick **handmade paper** sold at art stores is also strong and does not tear easily. Look around your house for old **magazines**, old **maps**, "junk" **mail**, used **envelopes**, leftover **wallpaper**, **newspapers** and **cardboard**. All these types of paper can be used for projects in this book.

OTHER SUPPLIES

PATTERNS

Some projects use patterns, which are in the *back of the book*. You can trace the patterns on tracing paper or writing paper, or you can use a copier to photocopy the patterns. A copy machine is a good way to make the pattern larger or smaller, if you want.

WHITE GLUE

White glue is stronger than glue sticks, but it wrinkles the paper, especially if the paper is thin. White glue mixed with water can be used instead of decoupage medium for some projects.

TAPE

Clear tape is an easy way to hold paper in place, but you'll want to use it only where it won't show. Double-stick tape (which is sticky on both sides) is handy to use for some projects, but you can roll up pieces of clear tape instead.

SPECIAL TOUCHES

Make your projects your way! Leave them plain if you like, or decorate them with glitter, fake gemstones, sequins, bits of ribbon and other fancy stuff!

BE CREATIVE!

If you don't have the exact materials in the supply list, use your imagination to find something else that will work just as well. For example, if the directions say to use ribbon, you could use string, raffia, yarn or embroidery floss instead.

GLUE STICK

Most of the projects use a glue stick for gluing the paper. This glue doesn't wrinkle most kinds of paper, it dries quickly and it's not very messy.

9

Bright Suncatchers

FILL YOUR WINDOWS with beautiful, bright colors, just like stained glass. Decorate your windows for each season or holiday, and let the sun shine in!

tip

You can make a set of suncatchers the same size as your own window panes to create your very own stained glass window.

SUPPLIES

paintbrush

spoon

clear plastic report cover

tempera paint

tissue paper

white glue

scissors

1. Pour white glue into a small cup or bowl. Add black tempera paint (or other color), and stir it with a spoon.

2. Cut the report cover on the fold. It's easy to trace a design or picture—just place it under the report cover and paint over the lines. Paint the outline of your design with a paintbrush and the glue mixture.

3. Let the lines dry. If you're in a hurry to finish, use a hair dryer. Pour white glue in a second cup or bowl and mix it with a little water to thin it.

4. Tear off the straight edges from the tissue paper. Tear the remaining paper into small pieces so that each piece has torn edges all around.

5. Paint a layer of the glue mixture over your design and add pieces of tissue paper. Paint more glue over the paper to make it shiny.

6. Fill in your design first, then add a background using a different color of tissue paper if you want.

MORE IDEAS!

• **THIS FLOWER** will make your window look like springtime!

● **THIS CAR WAS EASY TO DRAW.**
A photo of a car was placed underneath the
report cover and the lines were painted with
a pointy brush.

● **MAKE A WINDOW GARDEN**
by painting a different flower for
each window pane!

13

Friendship Baskets

WHY WRAP A GIFT or make a party favor when you can make a friendship basket instead? It's a gift that keeps giving because there are so many ways to use it. Make one for your locker or bedroom to hold all those small things that you don't want to lose.

TASSELS

Try using all different types of materials to make your tassels. Use colorful yarn, wire or ribbon and add beads, charms or buttons. Be creative!

SUPPLIES

tagboard

gift wrap or
colored paper

yarn, raffia
or wire

glue stick

Extras

• buttons
• beads and other
  decorations

scissors

hole punch

clear tape

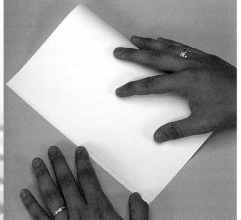

1. Fold a piece of tagboard in half widthwise.

2. Open the paper, then fold the bottom corners up to meet the middle fold.

3. Cut off the extra paper to make a triangle.

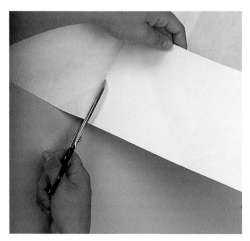

4. Open the triangle and use a glue stick to glue it to the back of a sheet of colored paper. Cut around the tagboard.

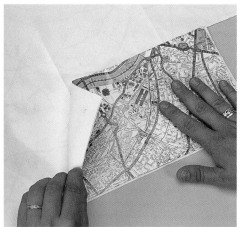

5. Glue colored paper to the other side of the tagboard so that both sides are covered. Cut around the tagboard.

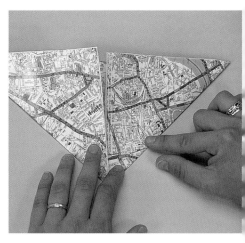

6. Fold the covered tagboard back into a triangle the way you did in step 2.

Make a basket chain! *Tie the handle of one basket from the bottom of another basket*

7. Tape the open edge of the triangle together. (Keep the top open, that's your basket.)

8. Punch a hole in each of the two corners, and tie on a piece of yarn, raffia or wire for a handle. Add beads or buttons to the loose ends for more decoration.

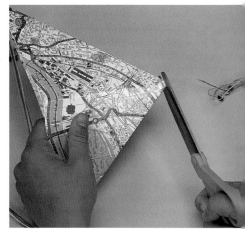

9. If you want a tassel on the bottom, snip off the tip of the triangle and thread through more raffia or yarn. Attach the end inside the basket with tape.

16

● **A WIRE HANDLE,** colored plastic beads and a yarn tassel are a perfect match to this fun basket.

● **BIG BUTTONS** make great tassel decorations for these baskets.

● **HANDMADE PAPER** and raffia from a craft store give this basket a natural look. The beads are polymer clay baked in the oven.

17

project 3 Magical Candles

CANDLELIGHT MAKES DINNERTIME SPECIAL. This votive candleholder is quick and easy to make, and the colors glow like magic when the candle is lit. You can make special candleholders for holidays and parties.

tip

To keep the tissue paper from tearing when being punched, sandwich the tissue paper between two sheets of copier paper.

SUPPLIES

tissue paper

glue stick

vellum or tracing paper

pencil

paper punch

glass votive candleholder or a drinking glass or jar with straight sides

scissors

1. Use scissors to cut tissue paper shapes for your candleholder. Or use decorative punches if you have them.

2. Use a glue stick to glue the shapes to your glass candleholder. You can overlap the shapes if you want.

3. Roll the candleholder on a sheet of vellum or tracing paper while marking the top and bottom edges of the area to be covered. Be sure you have traced enough to wrap all the way around the candleholder.

19

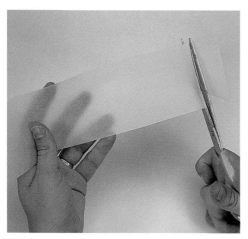

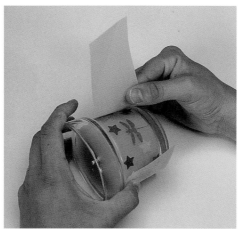

4. Cut the piece of vellum or tracing paper on the pencil lines. Be sure there's extra to overlap the ends.

5. Fit the paper tightly around the candleholder.

6. Overlap and glue the ends with a glue stick.

MORE IDEAS!

● **THESE SNOWFLAKES** were cut from ordinary white copier paper. The covering is tracing paper.

● **STRIPS OF TISSUE PAPER** were glued around a juice glass, then trees were stamped with a rubber stamp. Gold vellum paper was used instead of white for a warm golden glow!

● **OVERLAPPED CIRCLES** were cut from tissue paper to make this candleholder. It looks just right for a birthday party!

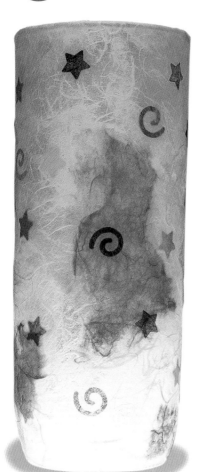

● **GIVE A CANDLE-HOLDER** as a great gift. It doesn't cost much at all!

● **REPEAT FAVORITE SHAPES** and colors to make your design look more artistic. These shapes were cut with scissors.

Mini Greeting Cards

Y OU'LL NEVER BUY ANOTHER GREETING CARD once you
see how easy it is to make them. This chapter will show you
three ways to make
cards that you'll be
proud to give.

SUPPLIES

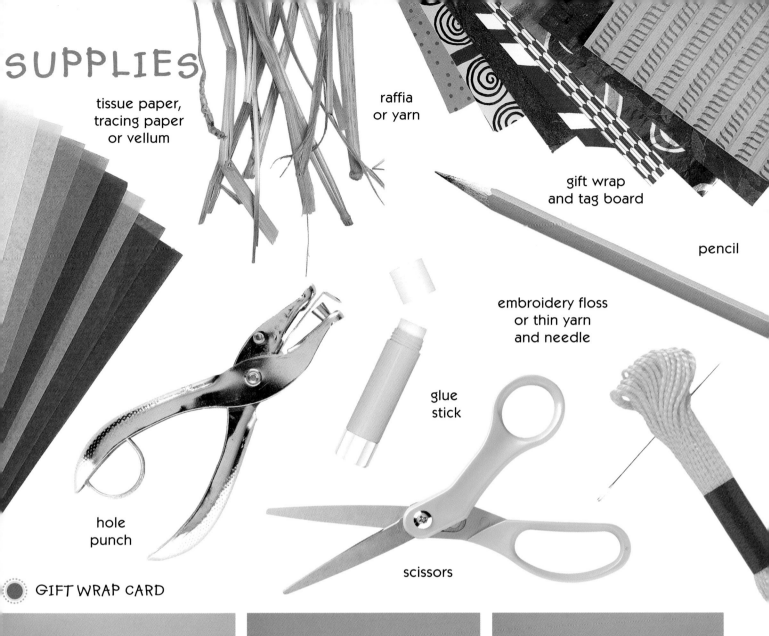

tissue paper,
tracing paper
or vellum

raffia
or yarn

gift wrap
and tag board

pencil

embroidery floss
or thin yarn
and needle

glue
stick

hole
punch

scissors

GIFT WRAP CARD

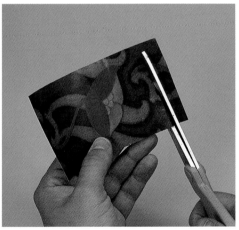

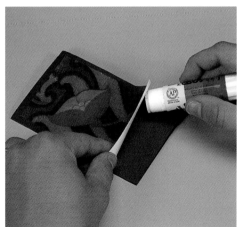

1. Fold a piece of tagboard or construction paper in half for the card. You can trim it to make your card any size.

2. Cut a piece of gift wrap or other decorated paper so it's just a little smaller than the card.

3. Put glue on the back of the gift wrap with a glue stick. Center the gift wrap on the front of card and stick it down. Open the card and use your best handwriting to write a message inside.

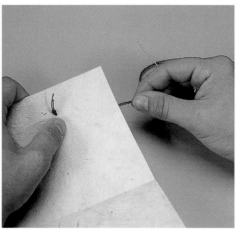

1. Fold a piece of paper for your card. Use paper that won't tear when it's sewn, such as thick handmade paper. Use a pencil to draw a design to sew.

2. Thread your needle with embroidery floss or thin yarn. Knot the end and sew up from the back at the beginning of your design.

3. Pull the needle and thread through the paper, then poke the needle down where you want the next stitch to be. Since this star has straight lines, each stitch will create one side of the star's arms.

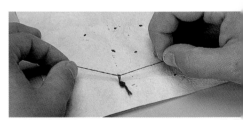

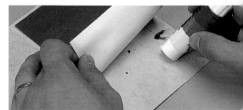

4. Keep going up and down through the paper with your needle and yarn.

5. Now you're almost finished. One more stitch to go!

6. After you sew the last stitch, knot the yarn on the back of the card. You can glue a piece of colored paper over the back of the design to hide the stitches. Write your greeting inside.

● TISSUE PAPER CARD

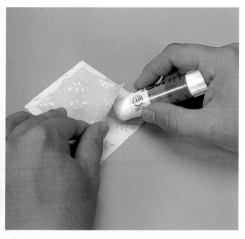
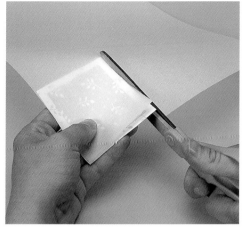
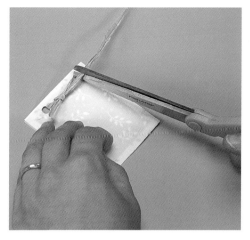

1. Use a glue stick to glue together a piece of gift wrap to a piece of tagboard the same size. Cut a smaller square from a different piece of gift wrap and glue that on top.

2. Cut a piece of tissue paper, tracing paper or vellum the same size as the tagboard.

3. Hold the tissue paper over the square of tagboard and punch two holes through all the layers. Use raffia or yarn to tie the layers together. Lift the tissue paper and write your message on the tagboard.

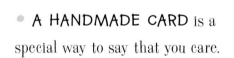

MORE IDEAS!

● **A HANDMADE CARD** is a special way to say that you care.

25

Button Up!

Y OU'LL FIND DOZENS OF WAYS to use this quick and easy button

envelope. Tuck a tiny card inside one to surprise a friend, or attach

a cord to make a purse. It is just the right size to keep in your school

notebook for holding paper clips, pictures of your friends, your lunch

money or other odds and ends.

● USE FUN BUTTONS,
ties and yarn to decorate
your envelopes.

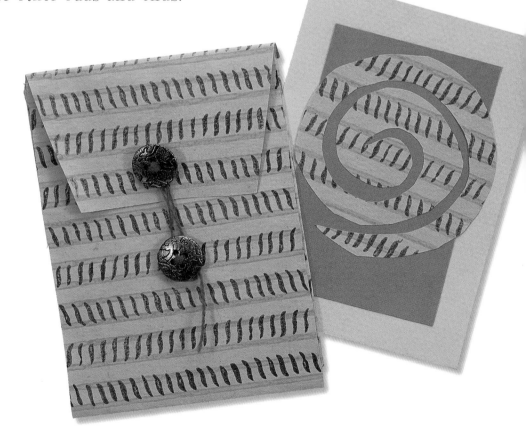

SUPPLIES

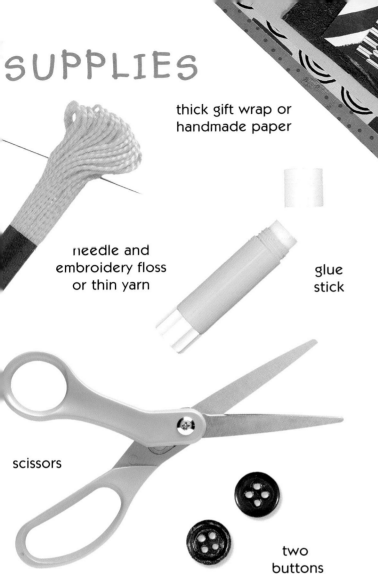

thick gift wrap or handmade paper

needle and embroidery floss or thin yarn

glue stick

scissors

two buttons

IF THE PAPER IS THIN, glue it onto a piece of brown paper bag the same size so it's strong enough to be sewn.

IT'S A GOOD IDEA to put a piece of clear tape on the back of the paper where the buttons will go. It keeps the paper from tearing.

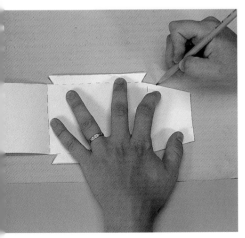

1. Trace or photocopy the button envelope pattern on page 60. Cut it out and trace it on the back of your paper. (Note: Read the tips above to be sure your paper is strong enough for this project.)

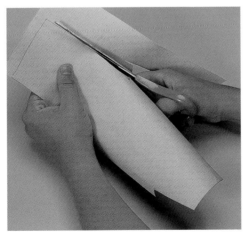

2. Use scissors to cut out the envelope.

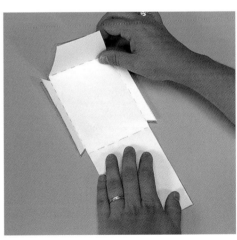

3. Use the pattern to fold the envelope at the dotted lines. Poke your needle through the paper where the dots appear on the pattern. These mark the two places on the envelope for the buttons.

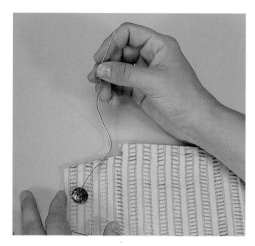

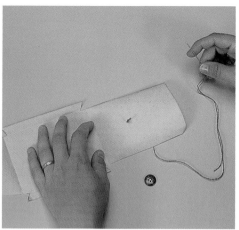

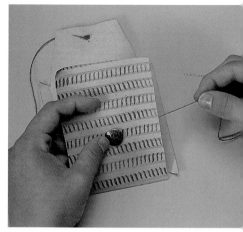

4. Use a needle with embroidery floss or thin yarn to sew on the top button. Start from the spot on the back of the short flap marked in step 3. Tie a knot leaving a 4" (10.2cm) "tail" on the outside.

5. Start the thread for the bottom button from the back of the long flap at the other spot you marked in step 3.

6. When you finish sewing the bottom button, tie a knot on the back and cut the threads without leaving any extra.

Get creative!! Handmade envelopes are **fun to decorate** and to send to friends!

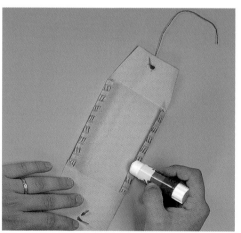

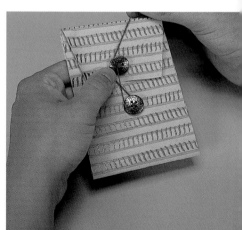

7. Fold the envelope where there are dotted lines on the pattern. If your envelope looks crooked, fold it again until it looks straight like the one above.

8. Use a glue stick to put glue on the two side tabs. Fold the envelope shut and press on the glued part with your fingers for ten seconds until it sticks.

9. To close your envelope, loop the thread "tail" from the top button around both buttons until all the thread is gone. Unwind it to open the envelope.

DON'T FORGET...

Use **strong** paper for this project. Test your paper first. Sew a few stitches in a small scrap to make sure the paper is strong enough to hold the sewn buttons.

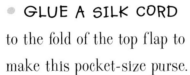

● **GLUE A SILK CORD** to the fold of the top flap to make this pocket-size purse.

● **A SCRAP OF WALLPAPER** was used to make this envelope. Wallpaper stores often give away old sample books, which can be used to make lots of paper projects.

29

Shining Stars

YOU CAN MAKE THESE FOLDED PAPER

STARS any size from all kinds of paper—

even aluminum foil and shiny candy

wrappers. Create "stained glass" stars from

vellum, tissue paper or tracing paper.

● **MAKE YOUR ROOM LOOK STARRY** and magical by hanging several stars from the ceiling. Punch a hole and tie yarn or ribbon to one of the points for hanging.

SUPPLIES

gift wrap or colored paper

glue stick

vellum

scissors

DON'T FORGET...

You can make stars from any kind of paper: newspaper, old magazines, wax paper, etc. Try anything ... try everything!

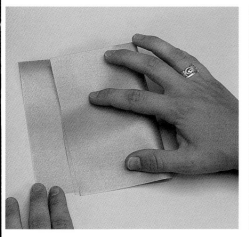

1. Fold a rectangular sheet of paper into fourths. This paper is vellum, but you can use any type of paper or foil for this project.

2. Cut on the folds to make four rectangles.

3. Fold each piece up from the bottom to make a triangle. Cut off the extra paper to make a square. You will need eight squares for each star.

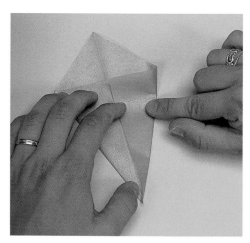

4. Lay a square on the table with the corner at the bottom and the fold going up the middle. Fold the left corner and then the right corner until they meet in the center. Crease the folds. Repeat this for all eight squares.

5. Lay one point sideways. Take another point and line up the bottom left edge with the other point's center fold. Use a glue stick to glue the point in place.

6. Glue the other points the same way. When you get to the last point, tuck it underneath the first point before you glue it.

MORE IDEAS!

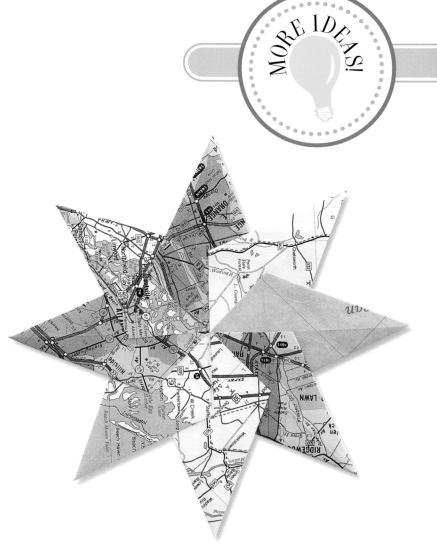

● THE STAR ON THE LEFT was made from gift wrap. The star on the right was made from an old map.

● **THIS RAINBOW FOR A WINDOW** was made with eight different colors of tissue paper. Tissue paper fades in the sun, so your star's colors will last longer if you choose a window that doesn't get direct sunlight.

● **STARS MAKE PRETTY ORNAMENTS.** This star was made from gold foil gift wrap.

Amazing Paper Beads

CAN YOU BELIEVE these colorful beads are made of paper and glue? You can make a whole pile in no time and then use them to make jewelry, tassels for your bookbag, or make a bead curtain for a window or doorway.

● **TRY COVERING** an old picture frame with all kinds of beads to make it look like new!

SUPPLIES

ROLLING PAPER BEADS

If you have trouble rolling the paper beads, roll the paper around a drinking straw or thin stick. Glue the tip of the bead and pull it off of the stick.

Use paper clips or wire to link beads together or string them on a cord to make a necklace.

gift wrap or other thin colored paper

Extras

- tracing paper
- clear nail polish

paper clips

scissors

glue stick

pencil

1. Trace or photocopy the triangle pattern from page 60 and cut it out. Use the pattern to trace a triangle onto thin colored paper.

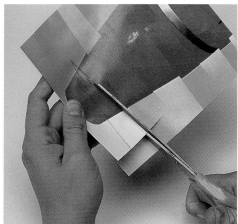

2. Cut out the triangle. If you want your beads to match, cut several triangles from the same piece of paper.

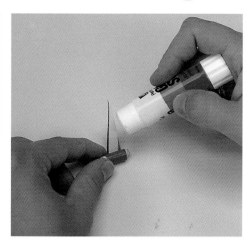

3. Start at the large end and roll the triangle into a bead. Glue the tip. If you want a shiny bead, slide it on a stick and paint it with clear nail polish.

Decoupage Fun

TEAR UP SOME PAPER, get out the glue and jazz up a picture frame with gift wrap. Decorate a lamp with a map or magazine photos or use see-through paper to make a glowing candleholder. Decoupage is easy to do and lots of fun!

• **USE AN OLD MAP** to decorate a lamp.

• **THIS CANDLE-HOLDER** was made from rice paper and tissue paper.

SUPPLIES

paintbrush

scissors

gift wrap
or other
colored paper

Extras:

• white paint

HEY KIDS....

Looking for other fun things to decoupage? Small gift boxes, notebook covers and round ornaments can all be turned into unique presents when decoupaged.

decoupage
medium or
white glue
mixed with
a little water

object to
decoupage

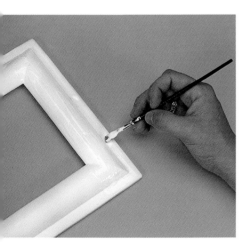

1. If you are using tissue paper on a dark object you may want to paint the object white so the paper colors stay bright.

2. Cut or tear the paper. You can decoupage any type of paper: magazines, maps, gift wrap, construction paper, tissue paper or paper bags.

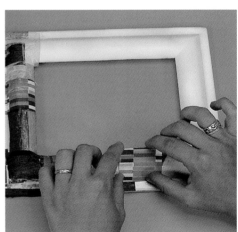

3. Paint the object with decoupage medium or white glue mixed with water. As you glue on paper pieces, paint more glue over them and smooth out any wrinkles with your paintbrush.

Festive Lanterns

SPECIAL OCCASIONS mean special

decorations, such as these paper

lanterns. You can make these lanterns

in colors to match your party supplies.

The tissue paper will glow if you hang

the lanterns near a ceiling light or a

sunny window.

tip

If you use solid-colored tissue paper for
your lantern, decorate it by cutting shapes
from other colors of tissue paper and
gluing them on with a glue stick. See
Magical Candles on page 18 for ideas.

SUPPLIES

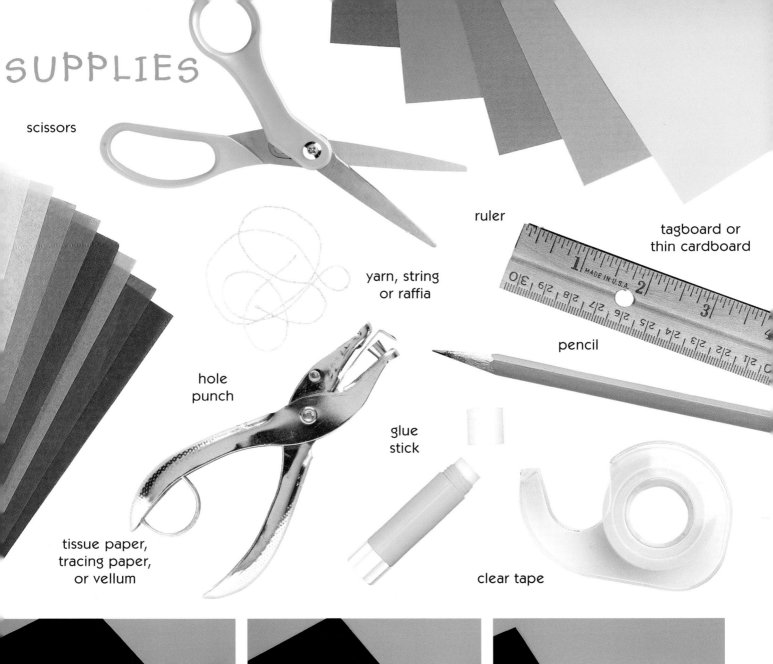

scissors

yarn, string or raffia

ruler

tagboard or thin cardboard

hole punch

pencil

tissue paper, tracing paper, or vellum

glue stick

clear tape

1. Fold two rectangular pieces of thin cardboard or tagboard in half widthwise.

2. On each folded piece make three marks 1" (2.5cm) from the edge on each of the four sides.

3. Draw a line to connect the three marks. Use your ruler to keep the lines straight on each side.

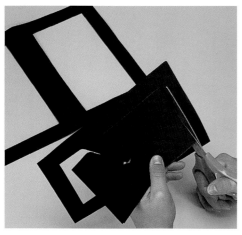

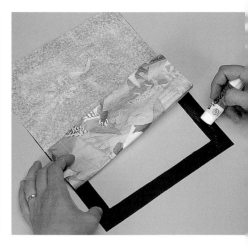

4. Cut on the lines without cutting through the borders. Unfold each rectangle. You should have two windows in each.

5. Trace the outside edges of each rectangle onto tissue paper, and cut on the lines. This is printed tissue paper, but you can use any type of paper that light can shine through.

6. Glue the tissue paper to the tagboard rectangles.

*Get creative! Make lanterns for your next party **and surprise** your **friends!***

7. Tape the sides of each rectangle together with clear tape so you have four windows in a row.

8. Tape the other sides together to make a box. This is your lantern.

9. Punch one hole in each of the four corners at the top with a hole punch.

10. Cut two pieces of yarn, string or raffia. Cross them in an X, and tie the ends to the holes. This is the hanger.

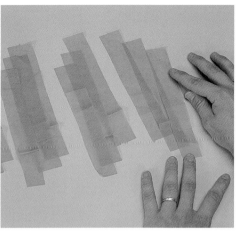

11. To make tassels, cut twelve 1" × 6" (2.5cm × 15.2cm) pieces of tissue paper and stack them in four groups.

12. Roll up each group and wrap clear tape around the top.

HEY KIDS... TRY THIS! Create four scenes from your **favorite cartoon or movie!**

13. Use scissors to cut the bottom half of each roll into thin strips.

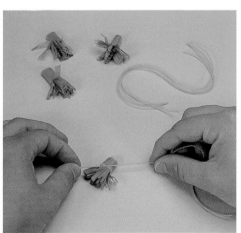

14. Tie a string or piece of yarn around each tassel.

15. Tape the ends of the strings to the four bottom corners of the lantern.

● STARS SHINE BRIGHT
on this pretty lantern. Choose
your own favorite things to
shine on your lantern. Perhaps
the sun, a rainbow or fireworks?
Use your imagination!

HEY KIDS! TRY THIS...

Use the Bright Suncatchers from Project 1 on page 10 to make a beautiful lantern that looks like stained glass! Just make four suncatchers, each a bit bigger than the windows in your lantern. Then tape the suncatchers inside each opening.

● PLAY WITH MANY COLORS

Each side of this lantern was cut from a different color of tagboard. Then the sides were stitched together with bright yellow yarn.

43

project **10**

Terrific Tags

Give the gift of your own creativity

by making quick and easy tags to tie onto

wrapped presents. This is a great way to use

up scraps of paper, gift wrap, old maps,

magazine photos or wallpaper.

TIP....

Look through magazines for different kinds of images that you can use on your tags. Mix lots of patterns for an interesting effect.

SUPPLIES

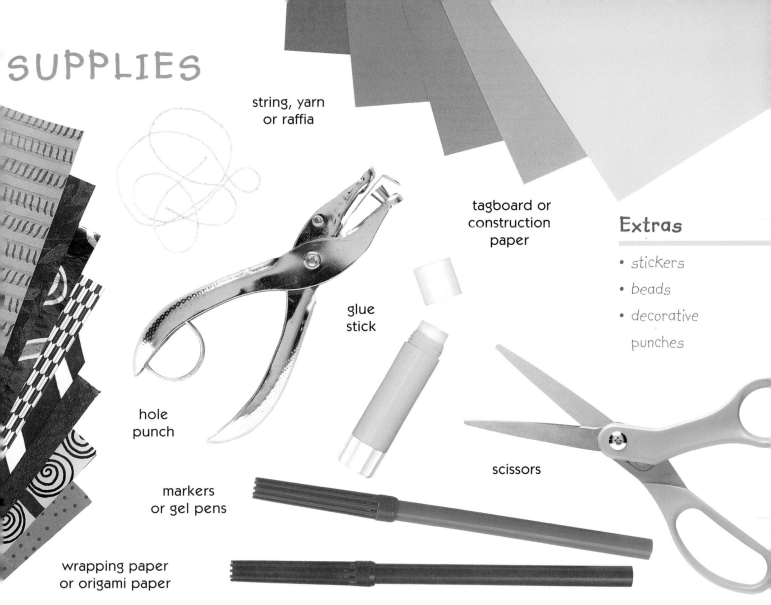

string, yarn
or raffia

tagboard or
construction
paper

glue
stick

hole
punch

markers
or gel pens

wrapping paper
or origami paper

scissors

Extras

- stickers
- beads
- decorative
  punches

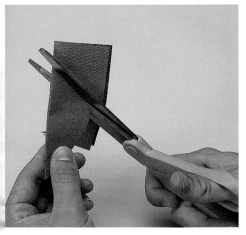

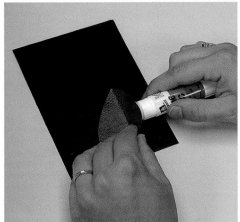

1. Cut out a piece of colored paper into the shape you want for your tag. This one will be heart shaped.

2. Glue this shape onto a piece of colored tagboard or construction paper.

3. Cut around the shape, leaving a thin border of tagboard.

4. Use a hole punch to make a hole in the top of the tag.

5. Loop string, raffia or yarn through the hole and knot the end.

6. If you want, write "To" and "From" on the inside. Gel pens look great on dark paper.

• **THESE TAGS WILL LOOK** pretty attached to holiday packages or a birthday gift.

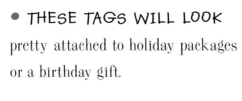

MORE IDEAS!

● HANG YOUR TAGS

on more than just gifts. These tags would look great on your backpack or used as a keychain.

● MIX AND MATCH

the paper and ties. Add beads, fake gemstones and other decorations to your tags. Get creative!

Party Streamers

NOTHING SAYS "PARTY" LIKE BRIGHTLY COLORED STREAMERS

on the walls and ceiling of a room. Make streamers in any shape you like

and use tissue paper that matches the

colors of your cups and plates. Taping

the pieces together takes no time at all,

especially if you use double-stick tape.

tip

Don't limit yourself to making streamers with only the patterns in the back of the book. Any simple shape will work if you alternate where the tape goes: middle, corners, middle, corners, etc.

● **THIS STREAMER USES**
the dragonfly pattern from page 61.

SUPPLIES

tracing paper

tissue paper

pencil

scissors

clear tape or double-stick tape

USE YOUR LEFTOVER PAPER

to make more party decorations, such as this fish. The scales were cut from scraps of tissue paper and glued in overlapping rows.

1. Trace and cut out the dragon-fly pattern on page 61. Cut tissue paper into sheets larger than the pattern. Make stacks of 4 to 5 sheets in the order you want the colors to appear. Trace the pattern onto the top sheet of each stack.

2. Hold one stack of paper together and cut out the shape. Then cut out the other sets of papers the same way. The more sets you make, the longer the streamer will be.

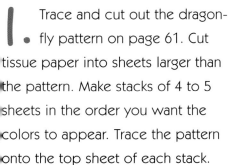

3. Put all the shapes in a pile. Put the the top piece of paper in front of you. Put a piece of double-stick tape or a piece of rolled-up clear tape in the center (the places marked "A" on the pattern).

49

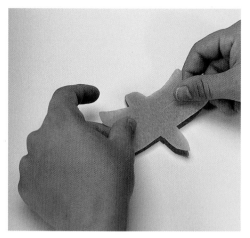
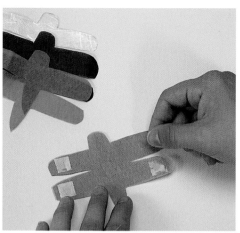
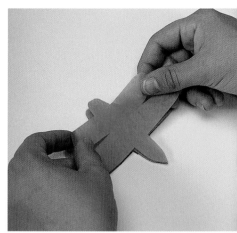

4. Put the second piece of tissue paper on top of the first piece.

5. Put double-stick tape on the second piece of tissue paper, at the places marked "B" on the pattern.

6. Put the third piece on top. Put tape on all the A places. With each piece of paper added, switch where you put the tape: A, B, A, B, until you have used all the tissue paper pieces.

MORE IDEAS!

• **STREAMERS FOLD FLAT** for storage, so you can use them over and over. This streamer uses the butterfly pattern from page 62.

● **THESE PATTERNS ARE FOUND**
on pages 61 and 62. Each pattern makes a
streamer with differently shaped openings.

● **THE RAINBOW
OF COLORS** makes
these streamers so
fun. Try using your
favorite colors.

Paper Mobiles

How CAN YOU DECORATE your room with a tree branch, string
and scraps of paper? Make a mobile! These butterflies will flutter
and dance beside an open window. You can also use stars,
hearts, fish, snowflakes—whatever
you can imagine.

KIDS! Try this!

FISHING SWIVELS will make
your mobile turn with just the slightest
breeze. They can be found in stores that
carry fishing tackle. FUN!

SUPPLIES

hole punch

gift wrap or colored paper

thread, yarn or fishing line

white glue

tree branch

scissors

pencil

fishing swivels

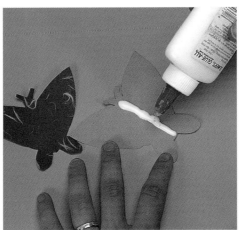

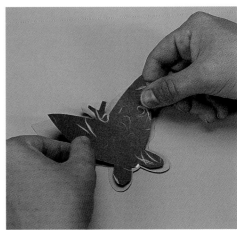

1. Trace or photocopy the two butterfly patterns from page 63. Cut out the shapes from two different colors of paper. If your paper has a pattern on just one side, glue another piece to the back.

2. Put a line of white glue down the middle of the large butterfly.

3. Put the small butterfly on top of the large one. While the glue is drying, make some more butterflies for your mobile.

4. Fold the wings of the smaller butterfly so they stand up.

5. Punch a hole or two anywhere you wish on the butterfly. Loop one end of a piece of fishing line, yarn or thread through the hole and knot it.

6. Tie the other end to the tree branch. For more movement, you can tie the line to a fishing swivel before attaching it to the branch. Hang your tree branch from the ceiling.

MORE IDEAS!

● **THIS MOBILE WAS MADE** with the dragonfly party streamer pattern on page 61.

● **FOR A WINTER WONDERLAND** cut out snowflakes using the pattern on page 63. Then cut on the dotted line. Join two snowflakes by putting the cut openings together and sliding the pieces toward each other. Decorate with glitter.

● **MOBILES CAN BE MADE WITH ANY SHAPE.** These aluminum foil and foil gift wrap stars were made following the directions on pages 31 and 32.

Star Books

When you open a star book, the pages make a perfect five-point star. It's amazing! You and your friends will want to make these tiny books for autographs, notes, jokes or very short diaries!

◀CLOSED
OPEN▶

● **HANG SEVERAL STAR BOOKS** as ornaments or party decorations, then give them as gifts to your friends and family.

SUPPLIES

gift wrap or other colored paper

scissors

solid-colored paper

glue stick

Extras

- double-stick tape

thin ribbon, string or yarn

thin cardboard

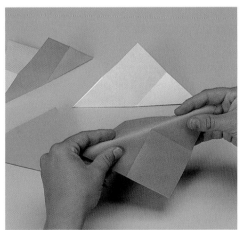

1. Cut five pieces of paper 5" (12.7cm) square. You can use paper of all one color or use five different colors. Fold each piece into fourths.

2. Open up a square and hold it with one corner in each hand and the other corners at the top and bottom.

3. Fold the paper back away from you diagonally so the top and bottom corners meet. Crease the fold with your fingers.

4. Open the paper and gently pop the center back with your thumb.

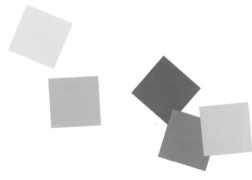

5. Bring the two side corners toward the center until they meet. Press them down and crease the edges to make a neat square. Repeat steps 2 to 5 with the other four squares of paper. These are the pages of your book.

6. Put the first folded page on the table in front of you with the opening facing you. Use a glue stick to put glue on the top part, then put the bottom of the next page on top. Put glue on top of the second page and put the third page on top, and so on until all five pages are glued together.

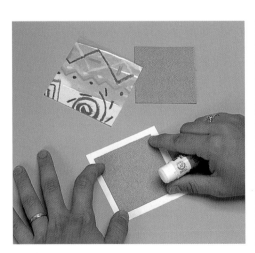

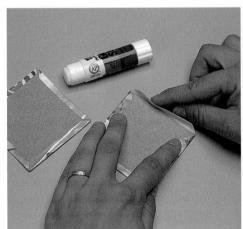

7. Cut two pieces of gift wrap 3½" (8.9cm) square and two pieces of thin cardboard 2¾" (6.9cm) square. Glue the cardboard in the center of the gift wrap.

8. Use scissors to cut off the corners of each square.

9. Glue down the edges of the paper with a glue stick.

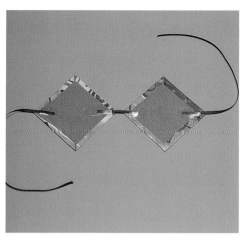  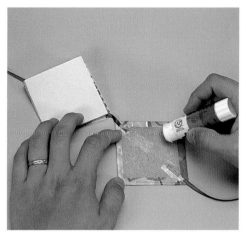

10. Cut two pieces of thin ribbon 2" (5cm) long, and use double-stick tape or a glue stick to attach them to the corners of the cardboard squares. Attach the two corners of cardboard together with a 1" (2.5cm) piece of ribbon.

11. Use the glue stick to put glue on one end of the pages. Stick it down on one piece of cardboard with the open pages pointing towards the longer ribbon.

12. Glue the other end of the pages to the other piece of cardboard. Close your book and hold it shut for a minute or put it underneath a heavy book until the glue dries.

MORE IDEAS!

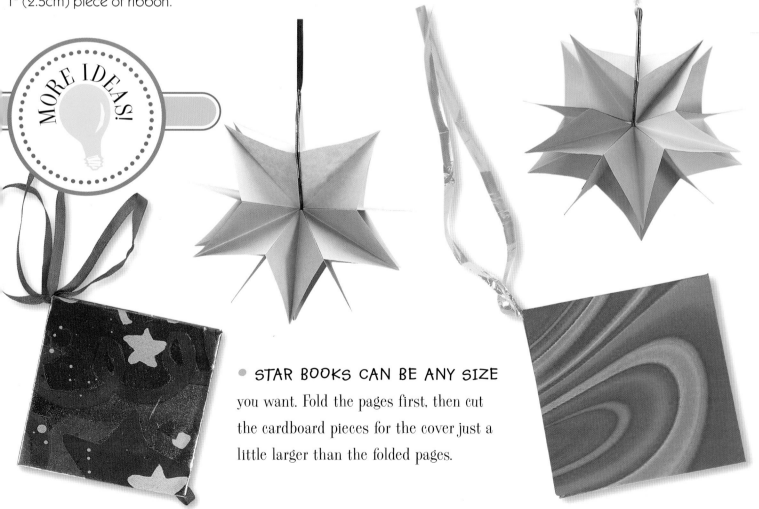

● **STAR BOOKS CAN BE ANY SIZE** you want. Fold the pages first, then cut the cardboard pieces for the cover just a little larger than the folded pages.

PATTERNS

THESE ARE THE PATTERNS for the Amazing Paper Beads project on page 34. You can use the long one for larger beads.

THIS IS THE PATTERN for the Button Up! project on page 26.

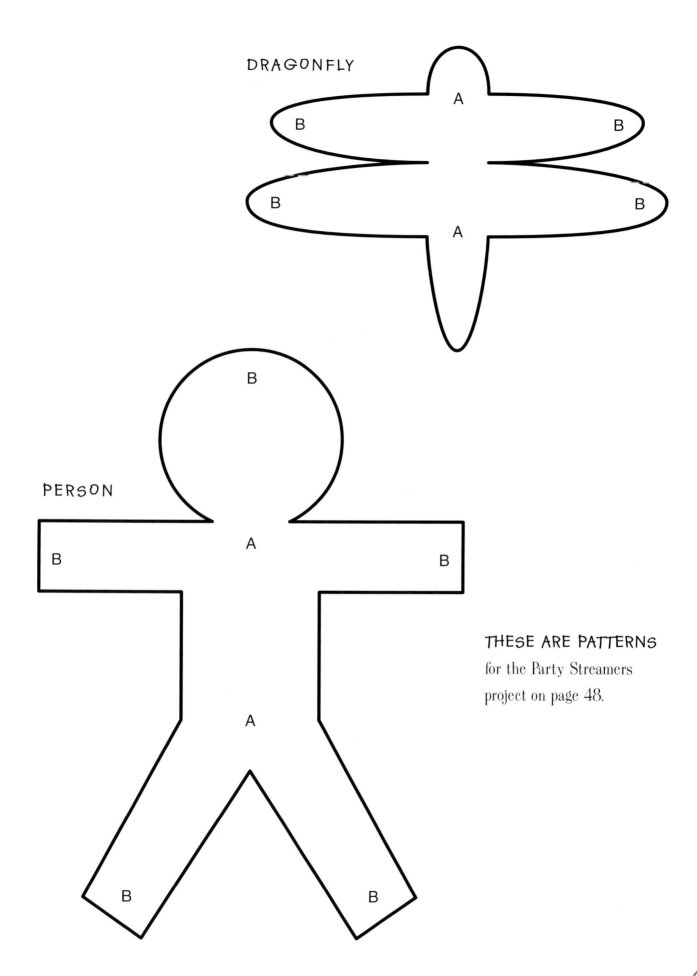

DRAGONFLY

PERSON

THESE ARE PATTERNS
for the Party Streamers
project on page 48.

PATTERNS, CONTINUED

STAR

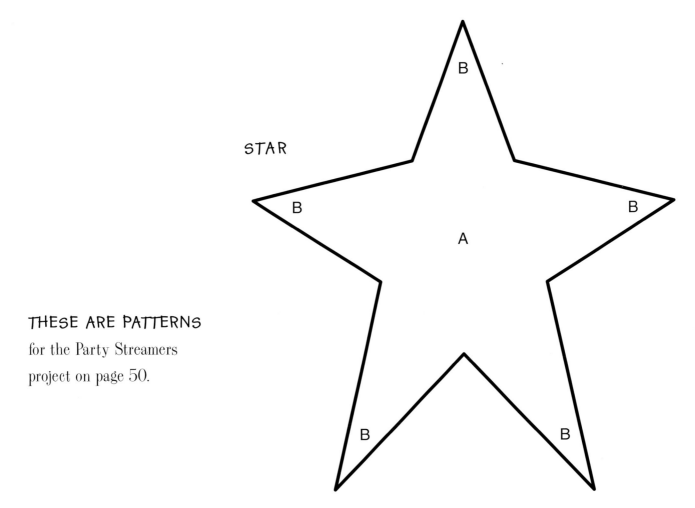

THESE ARE PATTERNS
for the Party Streamers
project on page 50.

BUTTERFLY

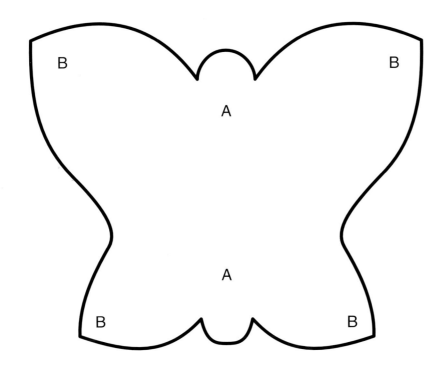

THESE ARE PATTERNS for the Paper Mobiles project on page 52.

THIS IS A PATTERN for the Paper Mobiles project on page 55.

More fun books for CREATIVE KIDS!

Try these fun, no-mess projects inspired by your favorite stories, including *How Many Bugs in a Box, I Wish I Were a Butterfly, Gingerbread Baby* and more. You'll learn how to make soft felt boxes, lace-wing butterfly barrettes, a milk carton gingerbread house and other exciting creations. There are 26 projects in each volume!

Volume 1: ISBN 1-58180-059-2, paperback, 128 pages, #31622-K

Volume 2: ISBN 1-58180-088-6, paperback, 128 pages, #31688-K

You can make incredible crafts using materials found just outside your window! Learn how to create pressed flower bookmarks, clay tiles, leaf prints, pebble mosaics, nature mobiles and souvenir pillows. You can use collected leaves, rocks, feathers and other natural treasures.

ISBN 1-58180-292-7, paperback, 64 pages, #32169-K

Create amazing creatures, incredible toys and wild gifts for your friends and family. All it takes is some paint, a few rocks and your imagination! Easy-to-follow pictures and instructions show you how to turn simple stones into something cool—racecars, bugs, lizards, teddy bears and more.

ISBN 1-58180-255-2, paperback, 64 pages, #32085-K